contents

introduction

Food technology is the use of science to improve the growing, harvesting, processing, packaging, distribution, cooking and storage of food. It makes use of the latest discoveries in science and the latest developments in technology.

The need for food The demand for food is rising rapidly, because the world's population is growing faster than ever. From the year 1500, it took about 300 years for the world's population to double to one billion. From 1800, it doubled again in only 130 years. By about 1975, only 45 years later, it had doubled again to 4 billion. There are now more than 6.6 billion people on Earth. The population is rising fastest in the developing world, where farming tends to be less productive and food technology is the most basic. Improvements in science and technology that could increase food production are most urgently needed in these places.

Modern farming is an industry that relies on high technology and big machines like this combine harvester.

NEW TECHNOLOGY

food technology

Ian Graham

Evans

Published by Evans Brothers Limited

© 2008 Evans Brothers Ltd

Evans Brothers Limited
2A Portman Mansions
Chiltern Street
London W1U 6NR

First published 2008

British Library Cataloguing in
    Publication Data
Graham, Ian, 1962-
    Food technology. - (New technology)
    1. Food industry and trade - Technological
    innovations - Juvenile literature
    I. Title
    664

    ISBN 978 0 2375 3425 7

Printed in China

Credits

Series Editor: Paul Humphrey
Editor: Gianna Williams
Designer: Keith Williams
Production: Jenny Mulvanny
Picture researchers: Rachel Tisdale
    and Laura Embriaco
Consultant: Chris W. Edwards,
    Head of Food and Dairy Technology,
    Reaseheath College

Acknowledgements
Title page: Scott Olson/Getty Images;
p.6 Malcolm Romain/istockphoto.com;
p.7 Robert Wallis/Corbis; p.9 Marco
Volpi/istockphoto.com; p.10 David
Gray/Reuters/Corbis; p.11 Scott Olson/Getty
Images; p.12 Eddie Cheng/EPA/Corbis;
p.13 Shaun Best/Reuters/Corbis; p.14 Ralph
Orlowski/Reuters/Corbis; p.15 Keith
Weller/USDA; pp.16 and 17 University of
Warwick; p.18 Floris Leeuwenberg/
The Cover Story/Corbis; p.19 Yoshisada
Nagasaka (National Agricultural Research
Center, Tsukuba, Japan) and Prof. Tony Grift
(University of Illinois, Dept. of Agricultural
and Biological Engineering, USA); p.20
Adeline Yeo/istockphoto.com; p.21 Chris
Jacobs/Columbia University; p.22 Natalie
Fobes/ Corbis; p.23 Sieto Verver/
istockphoto.com; p.24 Najlah Feanny/
Corbis SABA; p.25 Brian Prechtel/USDA;
p.26 Natalya Gerasimova/istockphoto.com;
p.27 Andrey Pustovoy/istockphoto.com;
p.28 Howard Sochurek/ Corbis; p.30 Purdue
University/LIBNA; p.31 US AIR FORCE/
Science Photo Library; p.32 Altrendo/Getty
Images; p.33 Gaurier/photocuisine/Corbis;
p.34 Chuck Savage/Corbis; p.35 Ed
Wheeler/Corbis; p.36 John Nordell/
The Christian Science Monitor/Getty
Images; p.37 Hotcan® Self-heating Meals;
p.38 Roderick Chen/First Light/Getty
Images; p.39 PASCAL GOETGHELUCK/
Science Photo Library; p.40 Richard Hobson/
istockphoto.com; p.41 PETER MENZEL/
Science Photo Library; p.42 Tony
Arruza/Corbis; p.43 Klaas Lingbeek van
Kranen/istockphoto.com

This book was prepared for
Evans Brothers Ltd by Discovery Books Ltd.

Food tech today The way our food is produced has changed a lot over the past few decades. Advances in genetics enable scientists to change plants and animals in order to improve the food made from them or reduce its cost. Advances in farming make it possible for fewer people to produce bigger crops from the same ground. New types of packaging keep food fresher for longer.

Do you trust food technology? Scientists can do amazing things with food. They can use nanotechnology to change it molecule by molecule to alter its flavour, texture or nutrition. They

This laboratory is producing seeds specially modified to suit growing conditions in India.

can treat it with radiation to kill germs or insects that would spoil it or cause disease. But all the clever science and technology counts for nothing if people will not buy the food. All new foods are thoroughly tested before they go on sale, but even so there is public concern about some of the ways in which science and technology is used to change food.

This book reveals the latest technology used in food production today and looks at the new food technology that is coming in the next few years.

CHAPTER 1
gene technology

The cells of living plants and animals contain a set of instructions, the genetic code, that controls the growth and development of the plant or animal. Scientists are learning how to change the genetic code to make better plants and animals for the food industry.

Breeding Farmers have been using genetics to change plants and animals for thousands of years without knowing it. They improved their plants and animals by breeding only from the biggest and best of them. This is called selective breeding. They also bred from different, but closely related, plants and animals. This is called cross-breeding or hybridisation. Farmers and growers have used cross-breeding for about 500 years.

DNA The genetic code inside living cells is made of DNA (deoxyribonucleic acid). The long, chain-like molecules of DNA are divided into chromosomes and the chromosomes are divided into units called genes. Genes control the production of proteins, and proteins build a plant or animal and carry out its functions. In the 1970s, scientists

Rod-like chromosomes made of DNA carry the genes that control an organism's growth and development.

Chromosomes

Strings of DNA form a chromosome

A cell

DNA code

One chromosome

discovered that all living organisms store genetic information in the same way. This meant that it should be possible to move genes from one plant or animal to another, and even from one species to another.

HOW IT WORKS

When scientists find a useful feature in a plant, they look for the gene that produces it. They cut the gene out of the plant's DNA and insert it into bacteria. Bacteria are used because they multiply quickly, making lots of copies of the new gene, and they are also very good at getting inside living cells. Common soil bacteria called *agrobacteria tumefaciens* are often used. Viruses are used too. The bacteria or viruses are allowed to infect the plant, or they may be injected straight into the plant cells by shooting them in with a special gun. Pieces of the plant containing cells with the new genes are then cut out and grown into new plants with the new genes. Transferring genes into animal cells is done by injecting the new genetic material directly into the nuclei of individual cells with a very fine needle.

GM crops Selective breeding and hybridisation take a long time and they often fail to produce the desired results. A farmer or grower can't be certain which genes will be passed on to the next generation. A new plant bred to have bigger fruit, for example, might also catch a disease more easily or rot faster. Scientists try to get rid of this uncertainty by transferring only the genes for the features they want. Plants and animals whose genes have been changed are known as genetically modified organisms (GMOs), and crops whose genes have been changed are also known as GM crops. The first GM

These potatoes come from a genetically modified crop.

WHAT'S NEXT?

Plants need water to survive and grow. By modifying plants genetically, it is possible to produce plants that need less water. This may enable crops to be grown in ground that would normally be too dry for them. In the early 2000s, Australia suffered the worst drought on record. Rivers dried to a trickle and farmland turned to dust. The wheat crop fell to less than half its normal yield. Field trials of wheat genetically modified to survive droughts better were carried out in Australia in 2007.

In Parkes, 300 kilometres from Sydney, Australia, land normally under water is cracked and baked by drought.

crop was a tobacco plant genetically modified to make it resistant to an antibiotic in 1983. The first commercial GM plant, a tomato, was created in 1994. The first GM product to go on sale in shops was a tomato paste made from GM tomatoes in 1996.

Which crops are GM? The most widespread GM crops are soya bean, maize (corn), cotton and oilseed rape (also known as canola). One reason for modifying them is to make them more resistant to pests so that less pest-killing chemicals have to be used on them.

Some crops are modified so that they are resistant to weed-killing chemicals. Chemicals can then be used to wipe out weeds without killing the crop.

By 2006, GM crops were growing on about 102 million hectares of land in 22 countries worldwide, with the area increasing at the rate of about 10 million hectares a year. The biggest GM crop is soya bean. More than two-thirds of all the world's soya beans are genetically modified.

Safe to eat? Producers of GM crops say they are safe, because they are thoroughly tested in laboratories and

FOR AND AGAINST

For
- Genetic modification produces drought-resistant and pest-resistant crops.
- Increases crop yields and so feeds more people.

Against
- Long term health effects unknown.
- May contaminate non-GM crops.
- Could change in unknown ways.

field trials. Critics say that GM crops are not necessary, because traditional breeding methods can produce all the food we need. Critics say the development of GM crops that resist powerful weed-killers and pesticides may lead to environmental damage from the chemicals or perhaps the appearance of super-pests and super-weeds. They also say there is a danger of GM crops causing unexpected reactions in people who eat them. One example they give is a variety of GM soya that was given a gene from Brazil nuts in 1995. Scientists testing the soya at the University of Nebraska, USA, discovered that people who were allergic to nuts were also allergic to the soya. The gene was removed. In 2005, research in Australia to develop a new pea plant with resistance to a pest called the pea weevil

These soya beans have been genetically modified to resist weed-killer, so that weeds can be killed without harming the crop.

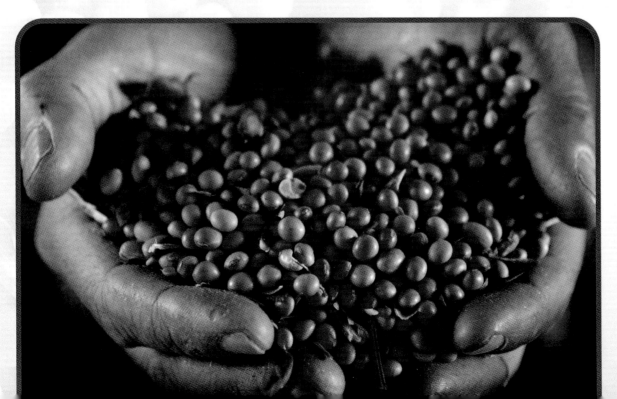

WHAT'S NEXT?

In 2006, scientists from the Harvard Medical School, the University of Missouri and the University of Pittsburgh Medical Centre announced that they had inserted a gene from tiny roundworms into pigs. The result was pigs that produced meat containing omega-3 fatty acids, which are good for the heart and circulation of people eating the meat. In the next few years, they will perfect their techniques in pigs and then move on to do the same thing in cows. It means that in future people with unhealthy fatty diets, which result in heart disease today, may be able to eat a healthier diet without having to give up all of their favourite bacon or steak.

was halted because the new peas caused lung problems in mice. GM producers say this shows that the testing system works.

Changing animals Deciding which farm animals should be allowed to breed together involves guesswork. If breeders had a genetic map of the animals, they could make selective breeding more scientific. They could develop tests to find out which animals have which genes. Then animals with useful genes could be bred together. The complete genetic map of an organism is called its genome. The genomes of the chicken and the cow have already been mapped. Others will follow.

Genetically modified pigs, sheep and cows have already been created. The first transgenic farm animals (animals with genes from another organism)

The pig with the yellow-green snout is a transgenic pig produced for medical research by adding protein from a jellyfish to its DNA.

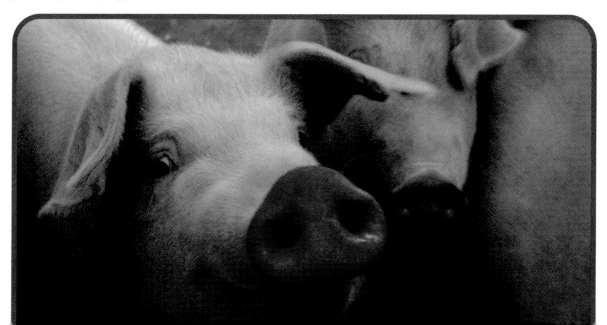

were produced for medical research. The first transgenic sheep, Tracy, was produced in Britain in 1991 by PPL Therapeutics. Its human genes produced milk containing human proteins for treating cystic fibrosis and emphysema in humans. The first transgenic pig was also produced in Britain, in 1992, by Imutran. Its cells had genetic 'flags', or markers, added to them that said 'I am human' instead of 'I am a pig'. Scientists hope this research will lead to transgenic pigs with organs that can be transplanted into humans. Rosie, the first transgenic cow, was produced in 1997. It produced milk with human protein that makes it safer than normal cow's milk for feeding to very young human babies.

Most genetically modified animals are still created for medical research. Dr Helen Sang at the Roslin Institute in Scotland has inserted human genes into hens so that they lay eggs containing cancer-fighting drugs. These drugs are usually produced in industry at great expense. In future, hens could be doing the work for the cost of a handful of corn every day.

GM foods on sale There is still a great deal of suspicion and caution amongst the public about GM foods. Meat and milk from GM animals and fresh GM fruit and vegetables are not on sale in the shops yet, but processed foods such as GM tomato paste are. Farm animals are sometimes given food made from GM crops. As a result of public concerns about GM foods some supermarkets will not sell food products from GM-fed animals.

People demonstrate their opposition to genetically modified organisms in street protests like this one in Montreal, Canada.

A German Greenpeace activist cuts off a sample of genetically modified maize plants in order to analyse it in a lab.

Do genes change by themselves?

Scientists don't always have to change an animal's genes. They sometimes stumble upon a lucky accident of nature. Plants and animals usually inherit half of their genes from each parent, so the genetic make-up of plants and animals is mixed in a different way with each new generation. In 2001, scientists in New Zealand found a cow, called Marge, with a gene that made it produce skimmed milk! Skimmed milk is healthier because it contains less fat than normal 'whole' milk. It is usually made by removing fat from whole milk. Butter made from whole milk has to be warmed after it is taken from a fridge before it will spread, but Marge's low-fat butter is spreadable straight from the fridge. Marge's calves were tested and they have the same gene. They produce low-fat milk too. The plan is to breed herds of cows with this same gene. The first low-fat milk and spreadable butter from them could be in the shops by 2011.

Tough tests In 2006, scientists in Australia developed genetic tests that can tell how tough a cow's meat will be to eat and even what the pattern of meat and fat, called marbling, will look like. Good marbling produces succulent cooked meat. A few hairs are plucked from the cow's tail and the DNA for the tests is extracted from the hair roots. In future, these tests will enable cattle breeders to improve the quality of meat on the dinner table by removing cattle from breeding programmes if tests show that they have the genes for tough meat.

This scientist at the US Meat Animal Research Centre in Nebraska, USA, is examining a farm animal's DNA.

Pharming Because of the public opposition to GM food crops, the next generation of GM farm crops will be grown to produce drugs and vaccines instead of food. This is known as pharming (from pharmaceutical farming). In 2006, genetically modified tobacco plants were developed in England to produce a drug that helps to prevent HIV. When the crop is harvested, the drug is collected. If the trial is a success, each plant will produce enough of the drug to protect an HIV sufferer for up to three months. It could be a way to supply cheap HIV drugs to African countries. More than half of the world's HIV sufferers live in Africa. Human trials of drugs produced from the plants could begin by 2009. The team is already looking for ways of increasing the drug output. One way is to grow the plants in water instead of soil. Instead of harvesting plants and crushing them to expose the drug, the drug simply diffuses into the water.

What is wrong with pharming?

Opponents of pharming worry that plants engineered to produce drugs could escape from greenhouses and alter wild plants, especially food crops. The greenhouses have to be airtight to stop dust-like pollen from the GM plants being blown outside on air currents.

CHAPTER 2
down on the farm

People have been farming for about 10,000 years. Farms and farming methods changed very little for most of that time. Now, developments in genetics, robotics and information technology mean that farms and farming methods are changing faster than ever.

SatNav and robots Traditional farming uses knowledge and experience built up over generations of working on the land. Today, farmers also use science and technology to make farms more efficient. Tractors fitted with satellite navigation can steer themselves around fields. They can use the same technology to make maps of the crop yield for each field, and then use this information to adjust the amount of fertiliser given to each part of a field. Some farmers are going even further and using robots.

Farm robots People have been replaced by robots and other machines in many industries. In car factories, for example, robots now do a lot of the work that was once done by people.

This robot is designed to cut grass. A group of robots will swarm over a field to ensure that all the grass is cut as quickly as possible.

The same is beginning to happen in farming. Robots are already cutting grass, picking fruit and milking cows on some farms.

A typical farm robot looks like a small car or buggy with no driver. Grass-cutting robots make a map of a field and then set off to cut the grass all by themselves. Robots for harvesting crops are more complicated. A fruit-picking robot makes a map of each tree and pinpoints the position of every piece of fruit. The robot's arms then use this information to reach out and gently pick the fruit. Vision Robotics in California, USA, are developing these fruit-picking robots. They started developing robots to pick oranges. Now, growers of crops ranging from cherries to asparagus are showing interest in using robots to harvest their crops too.

Rice robot In 2005, a rice-planting robot was tested in Japan by the National Agricultural Research Centre of the National Agriculture and Bio-oriented Research Organisation. It worked by laying mats of pre-planted rice seedlings in muddy paddy fields. Rice planting is a backbreaking job that few people are prepared to do today, so strong demand is expected for robots that can do the job.

This robot for picking mushrooms was developed at Warwick University, England.

WHAT'S NEXT?

The most difficult crops to pick are very soft crops like mushrooms, because they are so easily damaged. Scientists in Warwick, England, have built a robot that can pick mushrooms. It uses an arm with a suction cup on the end. It works more slowly than a human picker, but a robot can work 24 hours a day.

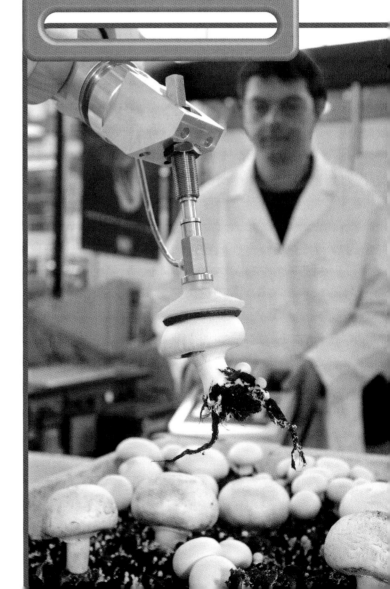

Milking robots Robots are already milking cows on some farms. Robot milking was developed in the Netherlands in the early 1990s. It was used in North America for the first time on a Canadian farm in 1998. Soon afterwards, a farm in Wisconsin became the first US farm to try the robots. Mason Dixon Farms in Gettysburg, Pennsylvania, USA, has installed ten robots to milk 500 of its 2,100 cows. Each robot does about 175 milkings every day. The robots have reduced the farm's labour costs by 75 per cent and increased milk production by 15 per cent.

Cows at the modern urban farm of Deltapark in Rotterdam, the Netherlands, are milked by robots.

HOW IT WORKS

When a cow comes to a milking station, the robot identifies the cow by reading an electronic tag on its collar. It finds the cow's udder by scanning the cow with a laser. The udder is then cleaned and suction tubes are attached. Suction draws the milk out and pipes it to a storage tank. If the robot has a problem, it can even call the farmer's mobile phone! By the end of 2006, only 1% of US dairy farms were using milking robots, mainly because farms invest in major machinery upgrades only every 10-20 years, but the numbers of robots used on farms are expected to increase rapidly.

The agricultural robot developed at the University of Illinois with its creators. 'Ag robots' have sensors to detect where a row of crops ends, then they automatically turn. The SICK logo refers to the company who has made the laser scanner for this robot, which helps guide it!

Global warming As farm animals digest food, they produce a gas called methane. Methane is a powerful greenhouse gas. When it is released into the air, it traps heat from the Sun and warms the atmosphere. There is great concern about how global warming is changing the Earth's weather. About one-fifth of all the methane produced worldwide comes from farm animals. Nearly all of the methane released in New Zealand comes from the country's 45 million sheep and 10 million cows.

WHAT'S NEXT?

Agricultural engineers at the University of Illinois, Urbana-Champaign, want to replace one big robot moving up and down a field with a team of smaller robots. It won't matter if one robot breaks down, because the others will take over its work. Small robots could reduce the amount of chemicals sprayed on farms. Instead of spraying a whole field, with chemicals drifting away elsewhere on the breeze, the robots will be able to 'spit' a tiny amount of chemical on an individual plant.

Turning down the gas Scientists in Perth, Australia, have made a vaccine that is injected into sheep to reduce the amount of methane they produce. Scientists in Belgium have found that adding fish oil to sheep food has the same effect. In New Zealand, a cow called Myrtle was fitted with a device that measured the amount of gas it 'released'. Then Myrtle was given different types of food. When Myrtle ate a plant called legume lotus, her methane output fell by nearly a fifth. A mixture of these and other methods may be used in future to reduce the greenhouse gases produced by farming.

Farming in the sky Future farms may be put in the middle of cities… in skyscrapers! Farming in a skyscraper is also called vertical farming. Vertical farms take up much less space than traditional farms. Professor Dickson Despommier and his students at Columbia University, who came up with the idea of the vertical farm, have worked out that a vertical farm producing enough food for 35,000 people would take up only one-300th of the ground needed for a normal farm. If funding can be found, the first experimental farm could be in operation within about 10 years.

Sheep release methane, a greenhouse gas that contributes to global warming.

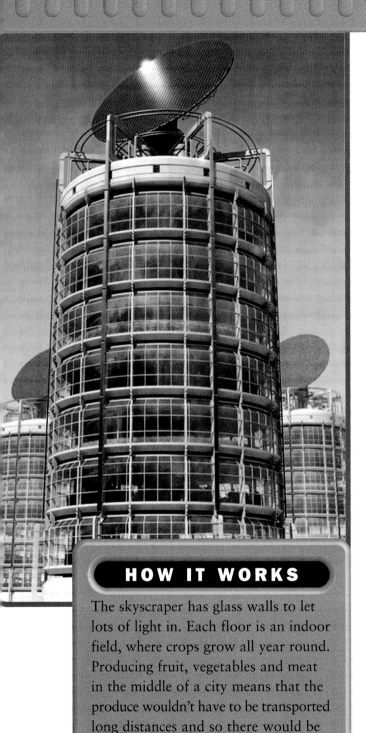

A future vertical farm might look like this glass tower.

HOW IT WORKS

The skyscraper has glass walls to let lots of light in. Each floor is an indoor field, where crops grow all year round. Producing fruit, vegetables and meat in the middle of a city means that the produce wouldn't have to be transported long distances and so there would be no transportation costs or air pollution from the big trucks normally used to transport farm produce.

Farms in the sea Most of the fish that people eat are wild fish caught by boats with nets or lines. The rest comes from fish farms. In future, more of the world's food needs will be met by fish farming, also known as aquaculture. The United Nations estimates that aquaculture will provide more than half of all the seafood we eat 25 years from now.

A fish farm is a set of floating cages containing fish. Sea water flows through the cages. Fish farms are set up in sheltered water near the seashore – in Norwegian fjords, and sea lochs on the coasts of Scotland and Canada.

Fish farms can reduce the price of fish that used to be very expensive, such as salmon. They can also make up for falling fish catches of popular fish, such as cod and herring. Fish catches are falling because of over-fishing and climate change.

Are there any problems with fish farms? Fish farms affect the plants, animals and water around them. Uneaten fish food and waste from the fish add nutrients to the water, which feed nearby plants and creatures. This alters the natural balance of life in the water. In addition, fish in the cages are so close together that pests and diseases spread easily from fish to fish. They can

Pests like this sea louse, attached to a salmon, can be a serious problem in fish farms.

infect wild fish too. Pests called sea lice are a problem in salmon. Wild salmon live in the sea, but return to freshwater rivers to spawn. Sea lice cannot live in fresh water, so they are not a serious problem in wild salmon. However, farmed salmon spend their whole life in seawater, which allows the lice to spread and multiply. They can also spread to wild salmon passing by. In one year, nearly all the wild salmon in one Norwegian fjord died because of sea lice. Wild salmon off the Canadian coast have been badly affected too.

Environmentally-friendly fish farming Scientists are developing new ways of farming fish that do not harm the environment. Scientists at the University of Miami, USA, have experimented with sinking fish cages far deeper than usual – as deep as

This fish farm floats in the calm, sheltered waters of a Norwegian fjord.

30 metres. Here, stronger currents flow through the cages and flush away uneaten food and waste that would normally collect underneath them. Researchers at the University of New Brunswick, Canada, are experimenting with 'self-cleaning' fish farms by mixing different species in the same farm. One species feeds on the waste of the next species. They found that mussels (shellfish) and kelp (seaweed) thrived near salmon cages and cleaned up their waste.

WHAT'S NEXT?

Future fish farms could be floating free at sea. In the open sea, the cages could be bigger and further apart. With more space between the fish, pests and diseases would not spread as easily. These fish farms would be able to move. They could sink deeper in the water if a storm or a ship came towards them. This sounds like science fiction, but work is already under way in Norway.

CHAPTER 3
functional foods

Most processed foods today are enriched or fortified with extra vitamins or minerals to make them more nutritious. Functional foods go one step further. They contain substances that help to improve health or prevent illness.

Nutraceuticals People have made claims about the health effects of foods for about 150 years. These early claims were unreliable because they were anecdotal – they relied on how well people said they felt after eating certain foods. Now, the health effects of foods and their ingredients can be tested scientifically. Some foods do have a good effect on people's health. Some of

Bread is commonly fortified with calcium, an important mineral for the formation and continuing strength of our bones.

them can even help to prevent serious illnesses. The substances added to foods to improve health are sometimes called nutraceuticals. The foods are also known as functional foods, designer foods, clever foods or techno-foods. Sales of these foods are growing rapidly. Many people like the idea of improving their health and preventing diseases by eating special foods instead of taking medicines. The term nutraceutical was invented in 1989 by Dr Stephen DeFelice. The word nutraceutical is used to describe a food ingredient or a food that is claimed to have a medicine-like effect.

This scientist is adding folate (folic acid or vitamin B9) to a dish of apple sauce. Folic acid is an important food supplement.

Early days Work on boosting the nutritional and health value of food began seriously in the 1930s. For good health, the human body needs the right amounts of protein, carbohydrates and fat, plus water and small amounts of vitamins and minerals. Even in wealthy developed countries in the 1930s, people had such a poor diet that serious illnesses and even deaths caused by vitamin and mineral deficiencies were common. So, vitamins and minerals were added to foods such as bread and breakfast cereals. Since then, many more foods have been fortified with extra vitamins or minerals. Vitamin D may be added to milk to prevent a disease called rickets that causes deformities in bones. Vitamin C and calcium are added to fruit juices. Vitamins B1 and B3, iron and calcium are added to flour.

Super-tomatoes Ordinary foods can be modified genetically or specially bred to transform them into foods with a good effect on health. Tomatoes are known to help prevent some cancers.

HELPING BABIES

A vitamin called folic acid is added to flour and bread in some countries, including the USA, Canada and Chile. It is added to help prevent problems called neural tube defects, which affect the development of a baby's brain and spinal cord. The effects of folic acid have been known for a long time, but surveys show that many women are still unaware of how important it is. Adding it to flour and bread ensures that everyone receives some.

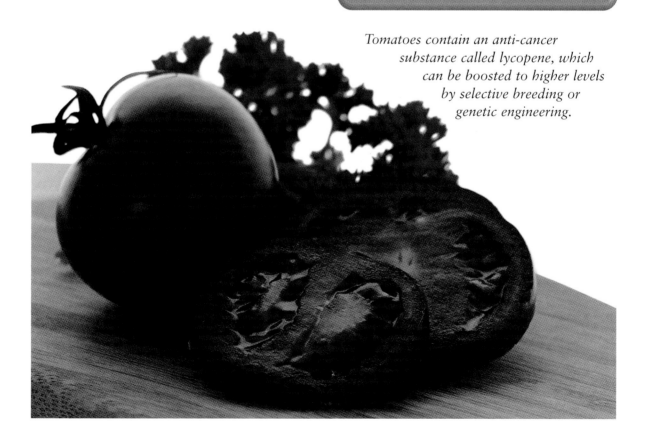

Tomatoes contain an anti-cancer substance called lycopene, which can be boosted to higher levels by selective breeding or genetic engineering.

One study found that men eating ten or more servings of tomatoes or tomato sauce every week lowered their risk of developing prostate cancer by 45 per cent. The substance in tomatoes that protects from cancer is called lycopene. It gives tomatoes their red colour. It is thought to protect cells in the body from damage. Cancer is caused by cells going wrong and multiplying out of control, producing a tumour. Protecting cells from damage may help to stop this uncontrolled growth from starting.

Now, a super-tomato has been developed with twice the normal amount of lycopene. It was developed in the Netherlands by selective breeding from different types of tomatoes with high levels of lycopene. It went on sale in Britain in 2006. Another high-lycopene tomato has been developed in the USA by researchers at Purdue University, Indiana, and the US Department of Agriculture. They used genetic engineering to boost the lycopene to more than three times normal levels. This tomato will probably not be in the shops for several years.

Brain food? One of the most popular dietary supplements today is omega-3. Research has found that omega-3 fatty acids reduce the risk of heart disease, lower blood pressure and help to stop

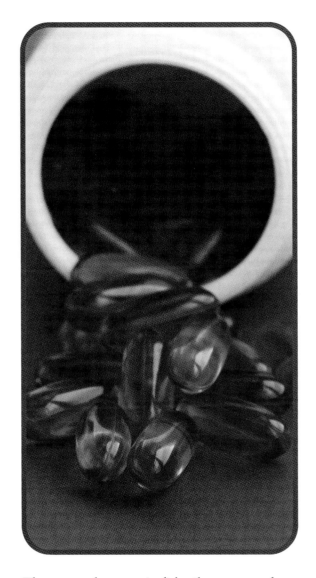

These capsules contain fish oil, a source of omega-3 fatty acids.

blood vessels from furring up inside. They also seem to help electrical signals travel from cell to cell in the brain. The body cannot make omega-3 fatty acids. They have to come from our diet. They are found in foods including oily fish such as mackerel, salmon, tuna and sardines. People are eating less oily fish

WHAT'S NEXT?

Today, functional foods deliver substances in food to the whole body. In future, perhaps using genetic engineering, it may be possible to target certain nutraceuticals at particular organs or tissues in the body, so that only those organs or tissues take them up.

today, so to make up for this, some margarines, yoghurts and eggs are enriched with extra omega-3.

Cutting cholesterol In the 1990s, research in Finland showed that substances called phytosterols, found in plants, could reduce a fat called cholesterol found in the blood. Cholesterol is essential for good health, but too much of the wrong sort of cholesterol can cause heart disease and clog arteries. Most cholesterol is made

This scan shows an artery which has become dangerously narrowed by a thick fatty lining, caused by high levels of cholesterol in the blood.

HOW IT WORKS

Nutraceuticals such as phytosterols are extracted from plants by dissolving them out. A solvent is mixed with mashed-up plants to dissolve the substance and wash it out of the plant. Different solvents dissolve different substances. Another method uses carbon dioxide gas. At about 800 times normal atmospheric pressure, carbon dioxide behaves like a liquid. The precise pressure and temperature are chosen to suit the substance to be extracted. When it is injected into a plant, it separates out the substance. This method is called supercritical fluid extraction.

PRE & PROBIOTICS

Prebiotics and probiotics are increasingly popular functional foods. They aim to improve digestion by acting on the bacteria in the gut. Food is digested by digestive juices produced by the body and bacteria in the gut. There are all sorts of bacteria. Some are good for digesting food. Others are not. The types and amounts of bacteria in the gut can be upset by illness, stress and some medicines. Prebiotics and probiotics claim to build up the numbers of good bacteria. Prebiotics are starchy substances that are not digested themselves, but they encourage the growth of good bacteria. Probiotics contain live bacteria that travel to the gut, where they help to digest food. Probiotics are often eaten in the form of yoghurts.

in the body, but some comes from food. The fatty diets that many people have today supply too much of the wrong type of cholesterol. Phytosterols reduce the amount of cholesterol absorbed from food by the blood, and so reduce the health problems it causes. Some margarines and yoghurts are now enriched with phytosterols.

Good or bad? Functional foods are not medicines, so they do not have to be tested like medicines. As a result, the scientific evidence for some of the

claims made for functional foods may be quite weak. Adding substances to foods to improve health or prevent illness is supported by many people, but many others are opposed to it. They say it amounts to mass medication. There are strict regulations covering the manufacturing and use of medicines, but governments have been very slow to issue regulations to control nutraceuticals and functional foods.

CHAPTER 4
nanotech

Nanotechnology is the technology of making and using particles so small that they can only be seen by using a powerful microscope. Nanotechnology is becoming increasing important – and controversial – in food technology.

Nanotechnology is already used to make hundreds of non-food products, including cosmetics and paints. Now, hundreds of companies all over the world are busy developing nano-products for the food industry.

'Nano' means one-billionth. The size of nano-particles is measured in nanometres, or billionths of a metre.

Nanotechnology makes use of particles up to about 100 nanometres across. You could fit 1,000 particles this size across the width of a human hair!

Nanotechnology is being developed in the food industry because it can make food safer by reducing the risks from harmful bacteria. It can also reduce the amount of fat that various foods contain without changing their flavour.

Nano-filters Liquids are often purified by running them through a filter so that solid particles are trapped by the filter. Nano-filters, filters made from nano-particles, are so incredibly fine that they even trap bacteria. Nano-filters are already being used to remove bacteria from milk. Nano-particles are also being developed to detect harmful bacteria in meat after it has been packaged. The particles are coated with

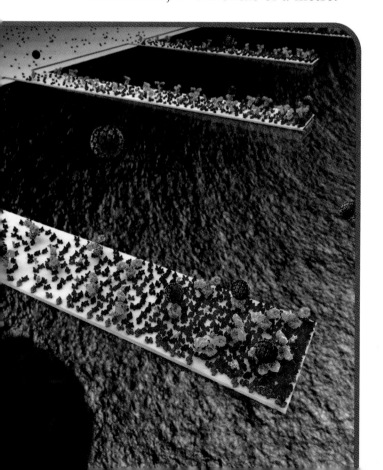

These tiny structures, like diving boards, are nanocantilevers. They could be used to detect dangerous substances, because they vibrate at different speeds when contaminants stick to them.

molecules that lock onto certain bacteria. When they link up with the right bacteria, they glow! So, the more harmful bacteria the nano-particles find and stick to, the brighter the glow.

Keeping clean Cleanliness is essential in places where food is processed. The surfaces food touches must be kept free of bacteria. This is done by washing them with bacteria-killing disinfectants. Using nanotechnology, it is possible to make surfaces that clean themselves. Nature discovered how to do this millions of years ago. The lotus plant has self-cleaning leaves. The waxy leaves are covered with microscopic bumps and hair-like structures. Water droplets roll off the leaves, collecting dirt and bacteria as they go. The secret of the lotus leaf was revealed in 2006

A drop of water sits on a water-repellent surface without being absorbed.

by researchers at the General Motors Research and Development Centre in Michigan, USA. Now nanotechnologists are developing self-cleaning surfaces for food processing, by copying the lotus leaf.

HOW IT WORKS

Scientists at the University of Twente in the Netherlands have made a copy of the lotus leaf by using lasers to bombard a surface with microscopic 'light bullets'. They carve a ripple pattern into the surface and make it water-resistant like a lotus leaf. The German chemical company, BASF, has developed a spray-on coating for surfaces that mimics the lotus leaf and makes them water-resistant or dirt-resistant. It is using the same coating to develop a water-repellent cardboard for food packaging, expected to be available by 2009.

Cabbage that tastes like chocolate? Hollow nano-particles can be filled with substances. This is called nano-encapsulation. A food can have nano-capsules added, containing a substance that gives the food a different flavour. Keeping the flavouring inside nano-capsules stops it from discolouring the food or reacting with it. Foods that children dislike could be given a more appetising flavour – cabbage that tastes of chocolate, for example!

Programmable food In 2000, NanoteK, a group of scientists from universities and research laboratories in several countries, embarked on a series of projects, including 'programmable food'. You decide its colour and flavour after you buy it!

In the future, programmable drinks will turn whatever flavour you choose. Researchers are also working on drinks which get thicker the more you shake them.

HOW IT WORKS

When you buy a programmable drink, it's clear and tasteless. At home, you put it in a new type of microwave unit or ultrasound unit. The drink contains nano-capsules full of different colours and flavours. Choose one microwave or ultrasound frequency and only the nano-capsules for red colour and strawberry flavour burst. Choose another frequency to get an orange drink, or coffee, or cola.

Reducing fat Reducing the amount of fat in food makes it healthier, but it also changes the flavour of the food and the way it feels in your mouth. Scientists in the Netherlands are using nanotechnology to reduce the amount of fat in food without changing its flavour or texture. They are making a new type of mayonnaise. Mayonnaise is usually a very fatty sauce. The fat is in the form of tiny droplets of oil. The Dutch scientists have created nano-droplets that are oil on the outside, but water inside.

Dangers? Nanotechnology can produce tastier, healthier food, but there may be risks too. Nano-particles are so small that they can get inside living cells. Once inside a cell, they can even move into the cell's nucleus, where its DNA is located. Scientists have already seen human cells with nano-particles inside the nucleus. The effects of nano-particles on DNA are unknown. Worries about possible health risks may put some people off eating nano-foods, just as they have been put off eating GM foods.

FOR AND AGAINST

For
- Nanotechnology can boost flavour, colour and nutrition.
- Can keep food fresher for longer.
- Can improve hygiene in factories.

Against
- Takes food further away from nature.
- Health effects unknown.
- Genetic effects unknown.

Mayonnaise made with nano-droplets of oil contains less fat than normal.

CHAPTER 5
packaging and preserving

Today food packaging is increasingly high-tech and clever. It can protect food from contamination, and keep food from spoiling for many years. It can even heat food up or cool food down when the package is opened. New labels can keep track of food with radio signals.

In the past, food was grown, harvested, processed and sold very quickly, because it didn't travel very far. It was often sold unwrapped. Today, food starts its journey to the table from all over the world. Good packaging is

Packaging is essential in the food industry today, to keep food clean and undamaged.

essential to protect it from damage and contamination, and keep it in good condition. Figures from the World Health Organisation show that food wastage in the developing world can be as high as 50 per cent, while good packaging reduces wastage in developed countries to three per cent or less.

Improving packaging Packets, cans and bottles contain much less material than they used to in the past. A drink can in the 1950s was more than four times heavier than the same can today. In the same time, a glass milk bottle has shed half of its weight. Plastic bottles are lighter too. Using less material to make each package and encouraging people to recycle as much packaging as possible saves energy and materials, and reduces the amount of waste that has to be disposed of.

Edible packaging One way to reduce the amount of food packaging waste is to eat the packaging! Dr Tara McHugh at the US Department of Agriculture (USDA) has developed edible packaging.

It could help to reduce the mountain of 1.8 million tonnes of waste that currently goes to US landfill sites every year. Even if the wrappers aren't eaten, they are completely biodegradable.

Active packaging Packaging that just wraps food is known as passive packaging. Packaging that uses special gases or chemistry to keep food fresher for longer is called active packaging.

Clever design and improved materials mean that plastic bottles contain a lot less plastic now than in the past.

HOW IT WORKS

The USDA edible packaging is made from a soup of mashed fruit or vegetables formed into sheets and dried to make a thin plastic-like film only a tenth of a millimetre thick. Cellulose and pectin, natural substances in fruit and vegetables, give the film its strength. So far, edible packaging has been made from apples, strawberries, peaches, carrots and broccoli.

MAP Food spoils, or 'goes off', because bugs and fungi grow on it and also because it reacts chemically with oxygen in the air. When meat, fish, fruit, vegetables and other foods that spoil quickly are packed, the air inside the package may be altered or replaced altogether with a different gas. Carbon dioxide and nitrogen are often used for this. Nitrogen is inert – it does not react chemically with food. Carbon dioxide slows down or prevents the growth of the fungi that make food 'mouldy'. Packaging where the air inside has been changed or replaced is called Modified Atmosphere Packaging (MAP). The mixture of gases used depends on the type of food.

A three-year-old sandwich The US Army has used MAP packaging and other techniques to produce a sandwich for soldiers on the move that stays fresh and edible at room temperature for three years! Substances called humectants are added to the filling to

Food packaging for astronauts needs to be rehydrated by pushing a needle through an opening in the top of the plastic package and injecting warm water.

WHAT'S NEXT?

With longer space flights envisaged for NASA astronauts in the coming decades, space food packaging is being improved and developed. Food prepared for Space Shuttle missions is designed to last over a month. Now NASA is developing two new food systems for missions in space that will last between three and five years. The meals used during space flights will be packaged and prepared in a similar way as those on the Shuttle. These meals are vacuum-packed or dried foods that are prepared simply by adding water. A second food system will be used on the surface of a planet or moon, where it is hoped that astronauts will be able to start growing and eating vegetables.

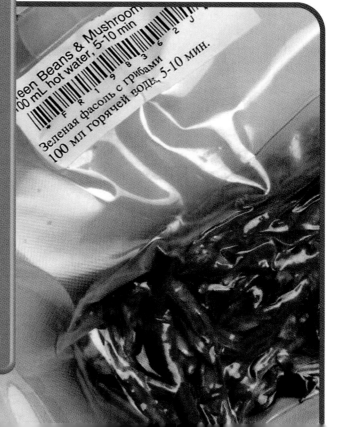

stop water from leaking out and making the sandwich soggy. Stopping water from leaking out also stops microbes from growing. Sachets of oxygen-absorbing chemicals mop up oxygen inside the foil wrapper, which stops yeasts from growing and spoiling the sandwich. NASA is very interested in this technology, because its Advanced Food Technology unit is trying to develop food with a shelf-life of up to five years for long space flights.

Hot and cold Some food packaging is passive until it is opened and then it becomes very active indeed. It may heat up the contents or cool them down.

Emergency food Self-heating food is useful for military forces and for providing emergency aid when cooking facilities are not available. During a humanitarian crisis in Lebanon in 2006, 200,000 self-heating meals were distributed to local people. Each meal is in a sealed pouch. Pushing it into a sleeve and adding a small amount of water activates a chemical mixture that heats the food to 70°C within about 10 minutes. The meals have a shelf life of three years and can be stored at room temperature.

A self-heating can provides a piping hot meal within a few minutes.

HOW IT WORKS

When a self-heating package is opened or activated, two substances mix together. A chemical reaction between them gives out heat, which warms the food or drink in the package. Self-cooling drink cans work like mini-fridges. They use the well-known scientific principle that a liquid needs energy to evaporate (change from liquid to gas). When a self-cooling can is opened, a coolant liquid inside a compartment quickly evaporates. The energy it needs to evaporate comes from the drink, which quickly cools down.

Preserving food with ultrasound

Food is often preserved in one way or another. It might be dehydrated (dried), salted, smoked, pickled, canned or bottled. Freezing is another common way to preserve food. Many foods cannot be frozen because they are damaged by the freezing and thawing process. Foods that contain a lot of water, such as soft fruit and vegetables, are damaged the most. Their cells burst when large ice crystals form inside them and expand when the food is thawed. In future, some of these foods may be frozen without damage by using ultrasound. Ultrasound is sound too high in pitch for us to hear. High-power ultrasound makes things shake.

Smart labels Packaging can now also keep track of food while it is being transported. The large packs used for transporting goods are labelled with what the goods are and where they are going. Today, these labels often have barcodes that can be read by a laser scanner. When the scanner is pointed at the package, it reads the pattern of black and white stripes in the barcode. This information is sent to a computer which records the product's

Large ice crystals damage food when it finally thaws. Ultrasound shaking ensures that only small crystals form on frozen food.

HOW IT WORKS

Research carried out at University College Dublin, in Ireland, has shown that food shaken ultrasonically, about 40,000 times a second, while it freezes suffers less damage. The shaking stops big ice crystals from forming. It shakes them apart. Small ice crystals do less damage to food. Ultrasonic shaking also produces numerous microscopic bubbles around which ice forms, speeding up the freezing process. The next step is to make ultrasonic freezers for the food industry, but this is probably still several years away. Further in the future, ultrasonic freezers may be used in the home.

details. Each product pack has a barcode too, that can be read by a scanner in a shop.

RFID A type of labelling called RFID goes one better. RFID stands for 'Radio Frequency IDentification'. An RFID tag on a package can be read from a distance by radio, even if the tag can't be seen. When the tag receives a radio signal, it sends back information about the product. RFID tags can be read automatically as packages enter or leave storerooms.

HOW IT WORKS

RFID chips consist of a plastic circuit printed onto foil and antennae for receiving and transmitting radio waves. Plastic circuits are cheaper than silicon, although at the moment they are also slower and store less data.

In future, more food products will have radio tags, like the one on this salmon, that can be read by a nearby scanner.

CHAPTER 6
science in the kitchen

In recent years, some chefs have worked with scientists to investigate the science of cooking. This kitchen science is also known as molecular gastronomy, or the science of deliciousness.

Cooking rules Most of the recipes used by cooks and chefs today were developed by trial and error decades, or even hundreds of years, ago. There are thousands of 'rules' about how food should be prepared and cooked, how long it should be cooked for, how hot it should be cooked, which ingredients go well with which other ingredients, and so on. Molecular gastronomy tests these 'rules' to find out which are right,

Food scientists are beginning to understand why foods like strawberries and cream go together so well.

which are wrong, and which can be improved by applying scientific principles. In this way, molecular gastronomy can make old recipes better and create new recipes.

Precision heating Meat is usually cooked at a very high temperature so that the heat passes through the meat and cooks the inside by just the right amount. By studying what happens to meat when it cooks, scientists found it was better to cook meat at a lower temperature for a much longer time.

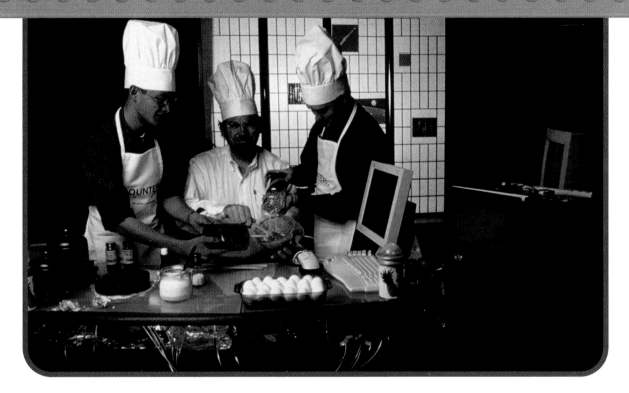

The temperature is very important. The perfect temperature is 58°C. At 58°C, a protein called collagen in the meat melts and makes it moist and tasty. At a higher temperature, collagen forms tight balls of tissue that make the meat harder and drier. At a lower temperature, bacteria are not killed and the meat could pass on infections and illnesses to anyone who eats it.

New kitchen technology

Traditional kitchen equipment can't provide the precise cooking temperatures and other requirements of molecular gastronomy. So, new kitchen technology is being developed. There are heating devices called thermal circulators that control the temperature of liquids to within a fraction of a degree. Vacuum

Future kitchens are as likely to have computer screens and high-tech utensils as they are to have mixing bowls.

sealers are used to encase meat, fish or vegetables in plastic, to seal in all their juices during cooking. High-pressure siphons transform any liquid into an edible foam, hot or cold. A device called an anti-griddle looks like a hot-plate, but it works in the opposite way – it quickly freezes anything placed on it. As well as freezing something solid, chefs use it to create dishes that are crunchily frozen on the outside and creamy inside. At the moment these devices are used only in a few professional kitchens, but equipment that was once used only by professionals, such as microwave ovens, often finds its way into kitchens at home.

conclusion

Some of the trends in food technology today give strong clues to how food may change in the near future. It remains to be seen, however, if consumers will accept – and eat – the new kinds of food that are developed.

Intensive farming In the second half of the twentieth century, farming advanced by using bigger machines in bigger fields to harvest more productive crops grown with the help of chemicals. Animals, too, are farmed more intensively than ever. In 1940, each farm worker produced enough food to supply 11 people. By 2002, that figure had increased to 90. As production increased, the cost of food fell. However, a growing number of people are unhappy with intensive farming. They don't like the unnatural way crops are grown and animals are kept. In addition, the huge amounts of animal waste produced on the biggest farms and the chemicals used on farmland can be washed off the land by rain and contaminate water in rivers and lakes. As a result, there is growing support for organic farming methods that are more natural and do not use man-made chemicals.

Intensive farming produces more food from a smaller area of land, but some people are unhappy with the conditions in which intensively farmed animals are kept.

Genetics Intensive or industrial farming will continue to use genetic engineering to improve plants and animals. Cloning will enable farmers to produce identical copies of their best animals. A clone is made by persuading a single cell of an animal to divide and grow into a new animal. This is the technology that was used in 1996 at the Roslin Institute in Scotland to produce Dolly the sheep, the first animal to be cloned from an adult cell. Using the same technology, the most productive farm animals could be multiplied hundreds of times over.

Will you eat cloned meat? In 2006, after a five year study, the US Food and Drug Administration (FDA) announced that meat and milk from cloned farm animals are safe for human consumption. They could be on sale in the USA within two or three years. The European Food Safety Authority (EFSA) is carrying out its own investigation, so meat and milk from cloned animals will take longer to reach the shops in Europe. Even if scientists and legislators decide that cloned meat is safe, it remains to be seen whether people will be happy to eat cloned animals.

If you don't eat jellyfish today, you might be eating it tomorrow! There are many edible animals and plants which we don't eat simply for cultural reasons.

WHAT'S NEXT?

We eat only a fraction of the plants and animals that could be eaten. In many parts of the world, people choose not to eat insects, snakes and a variety of seaweeds and sea creatures such as jellyfish. Making use of these would increase the food supply many times over.

glossary

antibiotic A substance that kills bacteria.

bacteria Microscopic living organisms that multiply by dividing. Some bacteria cause diseases.

cross-breeding Another name for hybridisation, breeding from two different varieties or breeds of the same species.

DNA Short for deoxyribonucleic acid, a molecule that contains the genetic instructions for how a living being lives and grows.

fjord A long narrow sea inlet between fingers of land.

functional food A food that does more than just provide nutrition, because it contains substances that improve health or prevent disease.

gene A small section of DNA, a unit of inheritance on a chromosome that passes characteristics from one generation to the next.

genome The complete genetic code of an organism.

GMO A Genetically Modified Organism, a plant or animal changed by genetic engineering.

hybrid The offspring of two different varieties or species of plants or animals.

molecule An atom or a group of atoms that forms the smallest unit of a substance.

nano One billionth (one thousandth of one millionth).

nanometre One billionth of a metre.

protein One of the chemical building blocks of living organisms, also an important part of a healthy diet eaten by people and animals.

sea loch A loch (Scottish lake) that connects with the sea.

species A distinctive group of plants or animals that share similar characteristics and breed with each other.

transgenic Having a gene, or genes, from a different organism.

virus A microscopically tiny piece of genetic material that is able to multiply only inside living cells. Viruses cause many diseases in plants, animals and people.

further information

Books

Freaky Food Experiments by Nick Arnold, Scholastic, 2007.

From DNA to GM Wheat by John Farndon, Heinemann Library, 2006.

Genetic Engineering: The Facts by Sally Morgan, Evans, 2003.

Nanotechnology by Rebecca L. Johnson, Lerner Books, 2006.

Sustainable Futures: Food for Life by John D. Baines, Evans, 2006.

Websites

The science of cooking
http://www.bbc.co.uk/science/hottopics/cooking

Ever Wondered About Food? Food science and cooking from the Open University
http://www.open2.net/everwonderedfood

What is molecular gastronomy?
http://www.discoverychannel.co.uk/science/kitchen_chemistry/molecular_gastronomy/index.shtml

Fish oils and brainpower
http://www.bbc.co.uk/science/humanbody/mind/articles/intelligenceandmemory/omega_three.shtml

Find out more about genes and genetic engineering
http://tiki.oneworld.net/genetics/home.html

The nanotechnology of mayonnaise
http://www.nanooze.org/english/articles/article8_nanofood.html

Find out more about fish farms
http://www.sciencenewsforkids.org/articles/20050511/Feature1.asp

Places to visit

Cadbury World,
Bournville, Birmingham B30 2LU
Tour a chocolate factory to see how chocolate is made.

The Museum of Brands, Packaging and Advertising, 2 Colville Mews, Lonsdale Road, Notting Hill, London W11 2AR
More than 12,000 items, including food packaging, from Victorian times to the present day.

The Science Museum, Exhibition Road, South Kensington, London SW7 2DD
One of the world's leading science museums, with exhibits covering agriculture, genetics and health.

index